JENNY HARRIS trained as a chef, then spent some time working in a bakery, where her interest in cake decoration began. She opened a shop just over six years ago to supply sugarcraft equipment, and all forms of celebration cakes.

SARA CARTER joined her four years ago and became a partner in the business. Both Jenny and Sara are gold medalists in their art and both teach at their local College of Further Education. Over the last three years they have produced many successful instructional videos in sugarcraft. Jenny now spends some of her time teaching and demonstrating abroad.

Cake Art

WORKSTATION

WORKSTATION *is a new concept comprising all the elements you need to begin the art of cake decorating.*

The first 48 pages of this book provide a beautifully illustrated introduction to this highly rewarding pastime, including ideas and projects for beginners to advanced. At the back of this book are 8 pages of templates, so you can practise and carry out the projects illustrated in the book.

Jenny Harris and Sara Carter

A DESIGN EYE BOOK

First published in 1995 by Design Eye Ltd.
The Corn Exchange, Market Square,
Bishops Stortford HERTS CM23 3XF

ISBN 1 872700 37 3

The Design Eye Team

Michael Tout
Lee Robinson
Aline Serra Littlejohn
Sally Symes
Joanne Coles

With thanks to our contributors
Dave Goodman and Pamela Hopkinson.
Photography by John Couzins.
Illustrations by Maxine Hamil.

Manufactured in China.

DEDICATION
Special thanks to both our families for their help,
support and criticism!

ACKNOWLEDGEMENTS
SEFCOL FOOD PRODUCTS LTD
Runcorn, Cheshire.
P.M.E. SUGARCRAFT SUPPLIES (HARROW) LTD
Middlesex.
WILLIAM LUSTY LTD
Runcorn.

CONTENTS

INTRODUCTION

Birthdays, weddings, anniversaries and celebrations of all kinds happen at some time in everybody's life – and a decorated cake is often the centrepiece of the event. What would a child's birthday party be if there was no cake with candles to blow out, or a wedding without a cake for bride and groom to cut?

Many people can bake a wonderful cake, but when it comes to decorating it, they often feel daunted by the special techniques and artistic skills that seem to be involved. Now, through the pages of this book, you can learn how to make and decorate cakes for every occasion.
With the help of the tools supplied with this Workstation and the patterns at the back of the book, each one of the projects will lead you gently forward, gradually increasing your skills and confidence. All the projects are designed to allow you to mix them around to suit a variety of occasions and colour schemes.

We do hope you will enjoy using this book and that your family and friends will delight in the beautifully decorated cakes you can make for all their special occasions from now on.
The marzipan and sugarpaste (rolled fondant) used for the cakes is available from supermarkets, sugarcraft shops or cookshops.
You can of course make your own, and we give recipes in the recipe section.

RECIPES

BASIC CAKE RECIPES

MADEIRA CAKE

YOU WILL NEED:

❀ 20cm/8in round or 18cm/7in square cake tin lined with greaseproof paper
❀ 250gm/9oz butter
❀ 250gm/9oz caster sugar
❀ 4 eggs, beaten
❀ 225gm/8oz self-raising flour
❀ 90gm/3oz plain flour

METHOD

1. Cream together the butter and sugar until white and fluffy.

2. Gradually beat in the eggs, adding a spoonful of flour from time to time to prevent the mixture separating.

3. Fold in the rest of the sifted flours, transfer the mixture to the tin and bake at 170c/325f/Gas mark 3 for approximately one hour.

4. Leave to cool in tin for 10 minutes then turn out onto a wire rack.

HANDY TIP

*For an alternative flavour,
add lemon or orange zest.
For chocolate flavour,
substitute 30gm/1oz of cocoa powder in place of
30gm/1oz flour.*

ℛich ℱruit Cake

Begin the day before by soaking all the ingredients below in half a cup of
brandy, sherry or orange juice overnight:

- ❀ 225gm/8oz sultanas
- ❀ 225gm/8oz raisins
- ❀ 125gm/4 ¹/₂oz minced dried apricots
- ❀ 125gm/4 ¹/₂oz currants
- ❀ 175gm/6oz glace cherries (halved)
- ❀ 50gm/2oz flaked almonds

YOU WILL NEED:
- ❀ 20cm/8in round or 18cm/7in square cake tin lined with brown parcel paper
- ❀ 225gm/8oz butter
- ❀ 225gm/8oz dark brown sugar (molasses is best)
- ❀ 4 eggs, beaten

Sift together the following ingredients:
- ❀ 50gm/2oz ground almonds
- ❀ 275gm/10oz plain flour
- ❀ 1 teasp 5ml mixed spice
- ❀ ¹/₂ teasp cinnamon
- ❀ ¹/₂ teasp ground mace
- ❀ ¹/₂ teasp ground nutmeg
- ❀ ¹/₄ teasp salt

METHOD

1. Cream together the butter and sugar.

2. Gradually add the 4 beaten eggs with a spoonful of the flour mixture to prevent separation.

3. Stir in the rest of the flour mixture then add the fruit.

4. Transfer the mixture to the prepared tin.

5. Bake for approximately 3 hours at 170c/325F/Gas mark 3. Individual ovens may vary.

ℋandy ℐip

BAKING CAKES OF DIFFERENT SHAPES AND SIZES

*To calculate how much cake mixture you will need when using tins of different sizes and shapes, follow this simple method. Fill your 20cm/8in cake tin with water up to where the mixture would go, then tip this into the different sized or shaped tin, repeat this process until the new tin is full.
The number of times you have done this is the number of times you need to multiply the recipe.*

𝒜PRICOT 𝒢LAZE

This quantity is sufficient for a 20cm/8in cake.

YOU WILL NEED:
❀ 250gm/9oz apricot jam
❀ 30ml/1fl oz water
❀ saucepan
❀ sieve
❀ pastry brush

METHOD

1. Mix the ingredients together in a small saucepan.

2. Bring to the boil.

3. Sieve the mixture. It is easier to brush on if used while still warm.

4. Store in a clean jar to use as required.

𝒢UM 𝒢LUE OR 𝒢LAZE

YOU WILL NEED:
❀ 1 teasp/5ml gum arabic
❀ 3 teasp/15ml water or rose water
❀ small bowl
❀ small jar

METHOD

*1. Place the water in the bowl and sprinkle the gum arabic
over the top.*

*2. Warm gently, either in a saucepan of hot water,
or in the microwave until the gum has dissolved.*

*3. Transfer to a small jar or bottle and
store in the refrigerator.*

Easy Sugarpaste / Rolled Fondant

YOU WILL NEED:
✿ 1 egg white at room temperature
✿ 30ml/1fl oz liquid glucose, slightly warm
✿ 500gm/1lb 2oz sifted icing sugar

METHOD

1. Place the egg white and glucose into a bowl.

2. Stir in as much icing sugar as possible, turn this mixture out onto a worksurface and knead in the rest of the sugar.

3. Continue to knead until the mixture is smooth.

4. Wrap well in cling-film and store in a sealable container in the refrigerator.

Marzipan

YOU WILL NEED:
✿ 250gm/9oz ground almonds
✿ 250gm/9oz icing sugar
✿ 1 teasp/5ml lemon juice
✿ 1 large egg white
✿ Almond essence to taste (optional)

METHOD

1. Sift together the almonds and sugar.

2. Gradually stir in the lemon juice and almond essence, if used.

3. Add sufficient egg white to the mixture to blend to a soft, pliable paste.

4. Wrap well in cling-film and store in a sealed container in the refrigerator.

FLOWER OR PETAL PASTE

This paste is used for modelling delicate flower petals and other fine work. Two recipes are given here, the traditional recipe and a quick version. You can also buy flower/petal pastes from sugarcraft and some cookshops, in powder form or as a readymade paste.

QUICK VERSION

YOU WILL NEED:
- 1 heaped teasp/5ml gum tragacanth
- 500gm/1lb 2oz commercial sugarpaste

METHOD

1. Knead gum tragacanth into the paste.

2. Wrap well in cling-film and place in an airtight container.

3. Leave for a couple of hours then use.

TRADITIONAL VERSION

This paste is more complicated to make but will enable you to get finer results. The paste is very tough to do by hand, and ideally it should be made in a food mixer - the freestanding, worktop kind - a hand-held mixer or a food processor will not do. Use a 5ml teaspoon to measure out the ingredients.

YOU WILL NEED:
- 500gm/1lb 2oz icing sugar
- 4 teasp/20ml gum tragacanth
- 2 teasp/10ml powdered gelatine
- 5 teasp/25ml water
- 2 teasp/10ml white fat
- 2 teasp/10ml liquid glucose
- 1 large egg white - at room temperature

MIXER METHOD

1 Sift together the icing sugar and gum tragacanth and warm them to blood heat (in the oven or microwave).

2. Sprinkle the powdered gelatine into the water and dissolve by placing the container in a saucepan of hot water.

3. Melt the fat and warm the glucose.

4. Place the warm sugar into the mixer bowl, add all the other ingredients. Using the beater, mix together on the slowest speed. Go up to the next speed and continue to mix until the paste is white and stringy in texture.

5. Place in a polythene bag, then into an airtight container and store in the refrigerator for 24 hours before using.

HANDMIXED METHOD

Proceed as 1-3 above.

4. Stir the liquids into half of the warm sugar, place rest of the sugar onto the worksurface.

5. Make a well in the centre, add the paste and knead the rest of the sugar into it.

6. Once it is all combined, pull and knead thoroughly until the paste is white and smooth.

7. Place into a polythene bag, then into an airtight container, store in the refrigerator for 24 hours before using.

ROYAL ICING

This classic icing forms a hard coating and is used as the base for other decorative techniques. It is also used for piping. Powdered egg albumen may be used instead of fresh egg white, follow the manufacturer's instructions.

YOU WILL NEED:
✿ 2 large egg whites
✿ 500gm/1lb 2oz sifted icing sugar
✿ A few drops of lemon juice (no more than ¼ teasp)
✿ 1 teasp/5ml glycerine - only add this if the icing is for the coating of the cake

METHOD

1. Place egg whites and lemon juice into a bowl.

2. Stir in enough icing sugar to give the consistency of double cream, stir briskly until smooth and white.

3. Continue to add icing sugar until the icing reaches 'soft peak' consistency. To test for soft peak, pull a spoonful of icing from the bowl and hold it up, the icing will retain its shape but just gently fold over at the top.

4. To store, place one layer of cling-film down onto the surface to exclude all the air, then seal across the top of the bowl with another piece of cling-film and if possible an airtight lid. This can then be placed in the refrigerator if not needed immediately.

Testing for 'soft peak' consistency.

PASTILLAGE

Pastillage will dry out and become very firm when exposed to the air. It is used for very rigid constructions, cake tops and some modelling.

YOU WILL NEED:
✿ Half of the quantity of royal icing given above
✿ 2 teasp/10ml gum tragacanth
✿ 500gm/1lb 2oz icing sugar (approximately)

METHOD
1. Take the royal icing and sprinkle it with the gum tragacanth, cover with a damp cloth. Leave for 30 minutes then stir the gum into the icing.

2. Sift approximately 500gm/1lb 2oz of icing sugar onto the worksurface, and make a well in the centre.

3. Put the royal icing mixture into the well and gradually knead in enough sugar to make a pliable paste about the same consistency as sugarpaste.

4. Wrap well and store as for sugarpaste.

HANDY TIP

Dry pieces flat on run-out film or polythene envelopes. This will stop the pastillage becoming distorted as it dries.

BASIC SKILLS

To achieve the best results when beginning the art of cake decorating, it is essential that you have the right equipment. A range of tools are shown here.

1 **Flower cutters**
2 **Modelling tools**
3 **Crimpers**
4 **Low turntable**
5 **Sprung blossom cutters**
6 **Selection of piping tubes**
7 **Piping bag stand**
8 **Stainless steel royal icing rule**
9 **Large rolling pin**
10 **Selection of plastic cutters**
11 **Straight side scraper**
12 **Small rolling pin**
13 **Palette knives**
14 **Sugar paste smoother**
15 **Tilting turntable**
16 **Garret frill cutter**

COLOURING ICING OR MARZIPAN

Use a paste colour if you wish to colour sugarpaste, petal/flower paste or marzipan. These colours are very strong so should be added to the paste a little at a time with the help of a cocktail stick and then kneaded in.

Keep adding paste until you reach the depth of colour required. Make sure the colour is well kneaded in so that it is not streaky. Test by cutting in half to make sure the colour is evenly distributed.

COLOURING ROYAL ICING

You can use liquid colour for this, but we recommend that, once again, you use paste colour. This gives good strong colours if required without changing the consistency of the icing. Add the colour bit by bit with a cocktail stick and stir in well until the desired colour is reached.

MAKING A PIPING BAG

A piping bag is a very important piece of equipment. You can buy nylon ones which need an adaptor in the end to hold the piping tube or nozzle, or you can make your own from greaseproof paper or greaseproof paper with a silicone finish (this is a little stronger). We prefer to make our own as they are easier to handle, and you may need several on the go at any one time.

1. Take a square piece of paper approximately 23cm/9in, fold and cut in half to make a triangle.

2. Roll point A over to point B then wrap round point B and take it up to point C. You should now have a cone shape.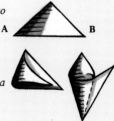

3. Fold the top points in and make two small tears in the top to secure.

4. You will need to cut about 2.5cm/1in off the bottom point to allow for the tube to go inside before filling with royal icing.

COVERING A CAKE WITH MARZIPAN

There are two methods depending on whether you are going to coat your cake with royal icing or sugarpaste. A 20cm/8in cake will need approximately 900gm/2lb.

METHOD FOR ROYAL ICING

1. Brush a ring of apricot glaze around the outside edge of the top of the cake.

2. Roll out a sausage of marzipan long enough to go around the top edge.

3. Press firmly into place with a palette knife on the inside.

4. Turn the cake over so that it is standing on the marzipan sausage. The flat base of the cake now becomes the top, working, surface.

5. Roll out the marzipan to 1cm/³⁄₈in thick - keeping the underside well dusted with icing sugar.

6. Brush the top of the cake with apricot glaze and turn it onto the marzipan, trim off all the way round and stand back the right way up, taking care not to dent the top.

7. With a piece of string, measure the circumference of your cake if round, if square measure one side only and multiply by four.

8. Roll out a strip of marzipan just over 6mm/¹⁄₄in thick to the length required, then trim to the depth of your cake.

9. Brush the marzipan with apricot glaze, lay your cake on its side on top of the marzipan and roll along the length, taking care not to dent the marzipan as you go, and making sure the top edge is level.

10. If your cake is square then, just do one side at a time, taking care to keep the corners square. Place on a cake board at least 5cm/2in larger than the cake.

12. Leave for several days before coating with royal icing. This will allow the marzipan to dry out so that almond oil will not seep through the icing and discolour it.

METHOD FOR SUGARPASTE: Follow the instructions as for royal icing up to step 5.

6. Measure the marzipan to ensure you have a piece large enough to go over the whole cake.

7. Brush the whole of the cake with apricot glaze.

8. Lift the marzipan and place it over the cake, gently easing in the sides. If the cake is square, ease the corners into place first, continue to ease until all of the cake is covered with no pleats or creases.

9. Smooth over with your hand and then use a plastic smoother.

10. Trim the bottom edge, and stand the cake on greaseproof paper until you are ready to coat it with sugarpaste.

COVERING A CAKE WITH ROYAL ICING

Coating with royal icing is not really difficult but it does need practice and having a turntable would help. Remember that you must add glycerine to your royal icing if it is to be used for covering a cake. You will need about 3 coats of royal icing to give a good finish. The second and third coats of icing should each be a little softer than the first. Allow time between coats for the icing to dry out well before you continue with the next coats.

METHOD
1. Place some icing on the top of your cake and with a palette knife, paddle backwards and forwards, spreading and smoothing as you go, this will also help to get rid of the air bubbles.

2. Once the icing is well spread over the top, then pull straight across with a straight-edged rule or large strong palette knife to give a smooth even top.

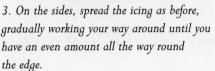

3. On the sides, spread the icing as before, gradually working your way around until you have an even amount all the way round the edge.

4. With a straight-sided scraper or rule pull around the side. At the same time, with your other hand, turn the cake until the sides are smooth all round.

5. If your cake is square, then coat one side at a time, working on alternate sides. Neaten up the corners with a sharp knife. Repeat this procedure for each coat.

Covering a Cake With Sugarpaste

If using a madeira cake there is no need to cover with marzipan first, just coat the cake with a thin layer of buttercream or jam.

YOU WILL NEED
✿ 750gm/1lb 10oz sugarpaste for a 20cm/8in cake
✿ Kirsch, brandy, or boiled water

METHOD
1. Knead the sugarpaste until it is soft and pliable.

2. Moisten the marzipan on your fruit cake with a little kirsch, brandy, or boiled water

3. Dust your work surface with icing sugar (some cookbooks recommend cornflour, but this is not advisable, it can react with the marzipan) and roll out the sugarpaste to between 6mm/¼in and 1cm/⅜in thick.

4. Pick up the sugarpaste and, keeping it icing sugar side down, place it over the cake and ease into place making sure that no air is trapped underneath.

5. Ease in the sides taking care not to stretch the paste too much.

6. When the icing is quite smooth, trim off any surplus from the bottom edge.

7. Using a smoother or your hand, smooth over and buff up to a shine.

Your cake is now ready for you to begin work on. Some of the projects we have designed must be started straight away, others would be better if the cake is left for a day or two for the icing to dry and form a harder surface.

ℳODELLING

*C*ontained in this chapter are the instructions for all the flowers, berries
and leaves used in the projects in this book.

YOU WILL NEED:
✿ The bone modelling tool ✿ A craft knife
✿ A modelling tool or a piece of wooden dowel with a pointed end
✿ Small fine bladed scissors ✿ A small plastic board and rolling pin ✿ The cutters from
the pack for Roses, Carnations, Blackberry flower, Primroses and Leaves
✿ Cardboard templates for orchids from the patterns at the back
✿ Petal/flower paste, coloured as desired ✿ Gum glue/glaze
✿ Cocktail sticks ✿ Tweezers - blunt ended ✿ Yellow cotton and sewing needle
✿ Wires and green tape from the pack ✿ Powder colours for dusting

𝒜CORNS

Colour pastes three shades of brown, one light, one mid-brown and one dark brown.

1. Using the palest colour, make a ball the size of a large pea - roll into an oval shape.

2. Pull a wire with a hook down through the centre.

3. Place a tiny piece of dark-brown paste over the hole left in the top by the wire. Leave to dry.

4. Glaze the acorn with several coats of gum glaze, leave to dry.

5. With mid-brown paste, take a small pea-sized piece and, with the bone tool, form into a cup shape.

6. Glue this onto the glazed acorn. It should not come more than one third of the way up the acorn.

7. With a cocktail stick, make indentations into the cup to texture it, and give it a natural look.

8. When everything is completely dry brush the cup with dark brown powder colour to give more texture.

ROSES

Use the largest of the blossom cutters from the pack.

1. Make a paste cone for the centre of the rose, the size should fit within one of the petals on the cutter.

2. Insert a wire with a hook. Pull through from the pointed end to the centre, leave until completely dry.

3. Roll out paste very thinly and cut out one blossom shape.

4. Place this in your hand and thin the edges with the bone tool.

5. Spread gum glue on the centre area and push the wired cone down through the middle.

6. Using the diagram as a guide coat petal 1 with glue and wrap tightly around the cone, repeat this with petal 3.

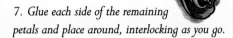

7. Glue each side of the remaining petals and place around, interlocking as you go.

8. Curve back the outer petals slightly. You may stop at this stage and go to Step 12 to complete, this forms a bud.

9. Cut another piece of paste and then remove petals no 2 and 4.

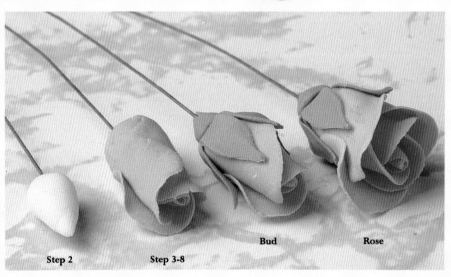

Step 2   Step 3-8   Bud   Rose

10. Place remaining petals in your hand, then thin edges as described in Step 4.

11. Glue the sides of these petals and add evenly to the rose so that they cover the joins of the previous row. Curve back and pinch to give a natural look.

12. Roll out some green paste very thinly and cut a calyx using the cutter from the pack. Glue and push onto the rose.

13. Make a small cone in green and insert the rose wire through thick end first and glue into position to form the hip.

SPRAY CARNATIONS

Use the large blossom cutter from the pack.

1. Make a hook in one end of the wire and cover with a tiny piece of paste, leave to dry.

2. Roll out paste very thinly and cut 3 shapes for each carnation, keep the shapes covered with a polythene bag whilst not in use.

3. Take one piece and with the craft knife go all the way round making small cuts in the outer edge.

4. With a cocktail stick frill the outer edge to give a fine ragged appearance.

5. Spread glue on the centre area and push the prepared wire through.

6. Fold in half over the wire.

7. Glue the centre $^1/_3$ and fold right hand section over to the middle.

8. Turn over and repeat Step 7. Squeeze the bottom of the flower together and leave this to dry completely.

9. For next layer repeat Steps 3 & 4, then glue the centre and insert the dry layer through the middle, gather the second piece around pinch to shape, leave to dry.

10. For third and final layer repeat exactly as layer 2.

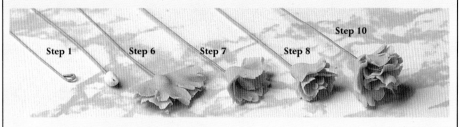

Step 1   Step 6   Step 7   Step 8   Step 10

11. To finish, with green colour paint a five point calyx on to the back of the carnation. In a spray use a variety of sizes, of one, two and three layer flowers.

PRIMROSES

1. Take a piece of yellow paste the size of a large pea.

2. Make a ball, Shape into cone, pinch out from the base to form a hat shape. This is called the 'Mexican Hat' method.

3. Place the small cutter over the top so that the point is central and cut out, then, with scissors, cut a V from the centre of each petal to make them heart shaped.

4. With a cocktail stick, thin the outer edges of each petal over your finger, or use the bone tool in the palm of your hand.

5. With the cocktail stick, indent the centre, put a small hook on one end of the wire, pass through the centre of the primrose - straight end first, pinch the flower onto the hook.

6. To make the calyx, using green paste and Mexican Hat method, cut a star shape using the template at the back. Push over a pointed tool or dowel and, with tweezers, pinch a ridge down from each point.

7. Push wired flower through centre and, using gum glue, fix onto the back of the flower, leaving the points standing away from the flower.

8. Brush a little deep yellow powder colour into the centre to finish.

BLACKBERRY FLOWERS

1. To make the stamen, thread a needle with yellow thread, wind this around a finger, 10-15 times.

2. Take thread off finger, twist into two then twist wire around the centre, leaving one end tiny as the stem, secure the cotton to the wire by stitching to the wire with the needle. Cut across top and trim to length required.

3. Using the Mexican Hat method, cut out white blossom with the small cutter.

4. Using the bone tool, and the palm of your hand as a mat, thin and cup each petal (without losing the point from the back).

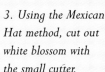
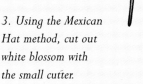

5. Pull wire with cotton stamens down through the centre until just the top of the stamen shows, pinch flower onto wire, leave to dry, then either paint a five point calyx or cut one in paste. Cut leaves using the leaf cutter in the pack.

ℬLACKBERRIES

Colour several small pieces of paste a variety of shades of green, and dark reds through to deep purple.

1. Make a ball of dark paste the size of a pea, insert a wire with a hook, leave to dry at least overnight.

3. Leave these to dry, then glaze. You will need more than one coat to get a good result.

4. Cut a small, flat star in green and push up under each berry. Glue into position.

2. Now make lots of tiny balls from the different coloured pastes and, using gum glue, stick them all over the larger ball.

ORCHIDS

CATTLEYA

1. Colour paste as required-retain a ball of white for the centres. More colour may be brushed on either before the flower is assembled or afterwards.

| Step 3 | Step 4 |

4. In main colour and leaf method, make 3 thin petals, thin edges with bone tool, vein down the centre, curve slightly in. Dry completely.

2. With white paste, take a piece the size of a pea, roll into a sausage shape 2cm/³⁄₄in long and insert wire with a flat hook. With the bone tool hollow out the front end and curve over, taper the end at the wire. Leave to dry completely.

5. To make centre petal, roll out main colour very thinly. Cut shape from template, frill and thin the outer edges with a cocktail stick, vein centre. Using gum glue stick centre petal around the dry centre, pinch edges together, then fold back front of petal. Leave to dry.

6. To wire the orchid together, take green tape and start around wire at the back of the

3. In main colour and using the same method as leaves (described opposite), make 2 broad petals, thin and frill outer edges with a cocktail stick, curve out, leave until completely dry.

central petal, then add the two broad petals either side to curve away from the centre, then add the three thin petals, one at the top and two at the bottom, to curve towards the centre, keep tape in one place throughout, do not move down the stem until all petals are in place, then tape to the end.

MINI OR QUICK ORCHID

These can be wired if you wish by inserting a straight wire into the centre before leaving it to dry. For the Celebration cake, we have made them without wire.

1. For the centre, take a tiny ball of white paste - roll a sausage shape tapered to a point at one end 1cm/³⁄₈in long. Leave to dry completely.

2. Roll out paste thinly-cut central petal shape from the template and treat as in cattleya orchid. Dry completely.

3. Using Mexican Hat method, cut out a five-point shape, using a calyx cutter or template.

4. Smooth and thin the edges with the bone tool. Curve one forward, curve petals either side of that back, and curve the two remaining petals forward.

5. Make a hole into the centre with tool or dowel, brush inside with gum glue and insert centre petal so that the broad part is between the two inward curving points. Dry completely.

6. Add powder colour as desired.

ℒEAVES

1. Roll out green paste to 6mm/¹⁄₄in thick then continue to roll, leaving a ridge down the centre, then roll out so the the ridge is only 1cm/³⁄₈in long.

2. With leaf cutter (or template) cut out so that the ridge is at the base of the leaf.

3. Dip a piece of wire into glue and push it into the ridge of paste.

4. Put in veins using a cocktail stick or by pressing onto the leaf veiner in the pack. Thin the edge and leave to dry on crumpled kitchen paper.

5. When completely dry, glaze well and use in flower sprays.

HOLLY BERRIES

Make small balls of red flower paste, dip a straight wire into gum glue and insert into the ball. Leave to dry then glaze. Use with holly leaves.

ROSE HIPS

Make as for acorns, using yellow flower paste, flatten top end slightly before inserting brown paste. Paint with red food colour to give a variety of shades. Glaze when dry.

TEDDY BEAR CAKE

A cake to appeal to the child in us all.

YOU WILL NEED:

❀ 20cm/8in cake on 30cm/12in board, coated in green sugar paste
and edged with green ribbon.
❀ Royal icing ❀ 125gm/4½oz quick flower paste ❀ Piping bags and No 1 tubes
❀ Crimper from pack ❀ Run-out film ❀ Templates from back of book
❀ Fine paint brush for painting detail on bears
❀ 125gm/4½oz quick flower paste (or flower paste)

TO DECORATE CAKE

*Any crimper work must be done immediately after coating the cake whilst the sugarpaste
is still soft.*

1. Cut a strip of paper the height and circumference of
the cake. Fold it into six, and cut to the curve
as shown at the back of the book.

2. Place this around cake and hold in place
with sticky tape.

3. Take the crimper and work around the paper pattern. To use the crimper, hold so that the ends are 1cm/³⁄₈in apart push into the sugarpaste and gently squeeze together. Release slightly and remove without pulling any paste away.

4. Turn paper slightly and use this as a guide

between the arches, crimp as before.

5. Remove paper and using the crimper again, work around the bottom edge of the cake. Rest the crimper on the board and push into the bottom of the cake, pinch, release slightly and remove. Then if you wish, continue the side pattern right down to the bottom.

6. Leave the cake to dry out, overnight is ideal.

7. Transfer pattern of bears and fence from the template by scribing through onto the cake

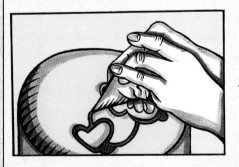

8. With a piping bag of brown royal icing and a No1 tube pipe the outline of the bear, making sure that all the lines are joined up.

Repeat this using darker brown for the fence.

9. Soften the icing with a little water so that when a trail is made across the surface it will disappear to a count of ten. Place into piping bags fitted with No1 tubes.

10. With this soft icing and in the appropriate colours flood in between the outlines one section at a time, allowing each section to dry slightly before you go on to the next one.

11. When bears are dry paint details.

12. Make butterfly wings in the same way but run them onto run-out film.

13. Cut out small blossoms in pink, blue and yellow flowerpaste.

14. With green royal icing, pipe grass on top and sides and fix blossoms as shown.

15. With the blue royal icing, pipe a line for each butterfly body, fix wings with the blue royal icing. (These may need support until dry.)

CHRISTENING CAKE

This cake makes a delightful centrepiece at any Christening feast, it will look just as pretty in pink or blue.

YOU WILL NEED:
For a 20cm/8in square cake on a 30cm/12in board

❀ 1kg/2.2lb sugar paste in yellow-the same in marzipan if it is a fruit cake
❀ 125gm/4½oz quick flower paste in white ❀ 125gm/4½oz Pastillage in white
❀ Template for crib and drape ❀ Smallest blossom cutter from pack
❀ Bonetool ❀ 3 plastic dowels
❀ A small amount of white royal icing in a piping bag with a No 1 tube
❀ A piece of foam sponge

IN ADVANCE

1. Roll out pastillage and cut out crib shapes. Dry base of crib over a curve. This will take 2 days to dry.

2. Roll some quick flower paste out really thinly, then cut out the blossom shapes, place them onto a piece of clean foam and press in the centre with the bone tool to give them shape.

3. Coat the cake board with a thin layer of sugar paste, trim edges neatly. Leave for 2 days. (It will stick on its own). Trim with ribbon.

4. Colour a small ball of flower paste, flesh colour, and roll into a baby's head shape. Dry on a cocktail stick.

5. When the crib pieces are dry, assemble with royal icing as diagram shows.

6. Leave to set, then make a pillow and a body shape. Fix into crib with royal icing. Brush baby's head with brown powder colour to resemble hair and fix onto pillow. Roll out rectangle of flower paste for the cover, frill the edges and fix into place as picture shows. Add blossoms to finish as picture shows.

TO DECORATE CAKE

1. Coat cake with lemon sugar paste. Fix onto board with royal icing, crimp around the bottom edge.

2. Divide each side of the cake into half and mark with a pin about 3cm/1¼in down from the top.

3. Roll out white quick flower paste very thinly and cut a shape using the template as a guide for drapes on the corners.

4. Drape over dowels as diagram shows and pinch one end together.

5. Drape up the corners of the cake, secure at the top with a little water. Repeat for all four corners.

6. In same colour paste cut strips 1cm/³⁄₈in wide, twist them and secure to the cake at corners over drape and at pin mark halfway around each side. Continue until all sides are complete.

7. Make the bows for each corner and each side centre by cutting a strip 1cm/³⁄₈in wide. Make 2 tails and fix into position using water or royal icing. Fold one piece to form bow and add a short piece over centre. Fix completed bow into place.

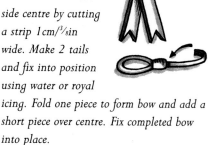

8. With white royal icing, fix crib into position and finish off the cake with the small blossoms and dots of royal icing as picture shows.

PRIMROSE CAKE

The delights of spring are reflected in this cake

YOU WILL NEED:

✿ 20cm/8in cake, coated in ivory and placed on 25cm/10in board also coated in ivory and edged with ribbon ✿ 125gm/4½oz yellow quick flower paste
✿ 125gm/4½oz ivory quick flower paste ✿125gm/4½oz green quick flower paste
✿ 125gm/4½oz brown pastillage ✿ approximately 30 primroses (See flower section)
✿ Green dried Gypsophilia ✿ Yellow and brown royal icing, piping bag and No 1 tube
✿ Frill cutter or scalloped pastry cutter

IN ADVANCE

1. Pipe yellow lace as in Two Tier Wedding Cake instructions.

2. Make basket by rolling out brown pastillage and mould it over a ramekin dish or similar to give shape. Trim and mark with a sharp tool to give basket effect. Leave to dry.

3. Roll out two strips of brown and twist together to form handle.

4. When basket is dry, add an extra strip around the top edge to neaten.

5. When all is completely dry fix handle into place with royal icing. Place a ball of sugar paste into the basket and arrange the primroses and dried Gypsophilia into this. Cut 6 leaves using template and green flower paste.

TO DECORATE THE CAKE

1. Crimp the bottom edge then leave to dry out, preferably overnight.

2. Cut a paper strip the same size as the side, fold into 6 and cut to a scalloped shape. With a pin, prick on the pattern as a guideline for your frill.

3. Roll the yellow paste out to no more than 3mm/⅛in thick.

4. Cut out the frill shape using a frill cutter approximately 8cm/3¼in wide. Alternatively, cut a circle with a scalloped pastry cutter. Cut out the centre with a circular plain cutter approximately 4cm/1½in wide.

5. With a cocktail stick roll and frill the outside edge.

6. Cut through the frill, paint a little water in the shape of your pattern on the side of the cake and stick the frill into place, trim to the required length, tuck under each end to neaten up, continue all the way round.

7. The second layer is done in exactly the same way using the same colour as the cake. When sticking the frill in place put it slightly above the yellow one.

8. To finish off the frill we have used a special wheel tool but a pastry wheel would give a similar effect.

9. Gently ease the lace pieces off the film, place two dots of royal icing onto the cake above the frill and fix the lace into position.

10. Fix the basket into position.

GEOMETRIC CAKE

The geometric design can be adapted to different occasions, such as graduation or retirement.

YOU WILL NEED:
✿ 20cm/8in square cake coated in white sugar paste
✿ 30cm/12in square board also coated in white sugar paste
and edged with white ribbon
✿ 125gm/4½oz pastillage ✿ Blue powder colour and a piece of foam sponge
✿ Royal icing half coloured white and half blue ✿ Piping bags and No 1 tubes
✿ Blue food colour pen

IN ADVANCE
In pastillage, rolled out thinly, cut the corner pieces, using the templates at the back of the book. Cut an oblong and form into a scroll shape. Leave to dry. Coat cake and board at least one day ahead before continuing.

TO DECORATE CAKE
1. Place cake onto board. With powder colour and dry foam sponge, gently stipple the entire surface of both cake and board. (This may need practice, so try it out on an old piece of sugar paste first).

2. Pipe a shell border in white with a No 1 tube around the bottom edge of cake.

3. Using template from the back of the book, scribe the pattern for blue piping onto cake.

4. With dark blue, pipe the same shell pattern onto the cake, following the pattern from the template.

5. Now position pastillage corner pieces, placing them 1cm/³⁄₈in away from the cake. Fix into place using royal icing. Prop them up until the icing dries.

6. When dry, pipe a shell border, as before, around the bottom edge and up the corners of each section, then on the tip of each corner piece in dark blue.

7. To complete scroll, pipe the initial you require and then with a food colour pen, write an appropriate message, or just indicate lettering with lines.

8. Fix scroll to top of cake with royal icing.

CLOWN CAKE

❋

This carnival cake will delight any child – or the young at heart.

YOU WILL NEED:

For a 30cm/12in oval cake on a 35cm/14in board

✿ 1m/1yd peach ribbon, 6mm/¼in wide

✿ 1kg/2.2lb peach coloured sugar paste (plus marzipan if fruit cake)

✿ 250 gm/9oz quick flower paste coloured red, yellow, blue, green, black, orange brown and peach ✿ Piping bag with a little brown royal icing and No 1 tube

✿ Garlic press ✿ Silicone paper

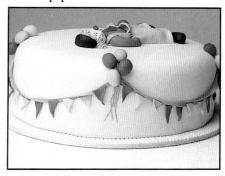

IN ADVANCE

Coat board with peach sugar paste, and indent with a cocktail stick 5cm/2in in around the outside edge to give pleated effect. Edge with ribbon.

TO DECORATE CAKE

1. Coat cake, keep bottom edge very straight and neat, fix to board.

2. Divide cake evenly into four and mark top edge with a pin.

3. Make bas-relief clown on top of cake. Trace clown outline from the back of the book onto silicone paper.

4. With the paste mixture on the paper make a padding for the body and trousers of the clown tapering down at the edges, using the traced design as your guide for size.

5. Make the arms in flesh colour, again using the paper and traced design as a guide.

6. Transfer all these pieces to the cake using a little water as the glue.

7. For socks, roll a sausage shape of paste and position.

8. For shoes, mould black paste to shoe shape and position.

9. For shirt, roll paste out very thinly and cut to shape, you can use the traced design as a guide, remember to allow for the padding.

10. Fit the shirt shape over the padding. Fold the edges under so that no padding shows and the shirt appears to go around the body.

11. For trousers use thin paste cut to shape and place over padding as for shirt then ease the top of the trousers out to give a baggy appearance.

12. With thin paste cut the tie and position.

13. Cut very thin strips for the braces and fix in position with a tiny spot of royal icing (do these after the trousers are dry).

14. With flesh coloured paste make a rugby ball shape for the head, position and flatten slightly. When dry paint on facial details and stick on a red paste nose.

15. For hair use orange paste and squeeze through a garlic press. Cut off and fix to head.

16. Model a hat from black paste.

17. Cut thin strips of brown flower paste twist slightly and drape around the sides. Secure at the 4 division marks. Cut out triangular flags in Red, Yellow, Green and Blue and stick to the brown rope with gum glue, to make the bunting.

18. Roll small balls of paste in these 4 colours into balloon shapes and stick into position with royal icing, pipe strings for balloons to complete.

GOLDEN WEDDING CAKE

This lovely cream and gold cake is suitable for a golden wedding or golden birthday celebration.

YOU WILL NEED:
For a 20cm/8in square cake

❀ 35cm/14in square gold cake board
❀ 1kg/2.2lb dark cream sugar paste plus marzipan if fruit cake
❀ 125gm/4½oz pastillage (cream) ❀ 125gm/4½oz quick flower paste
❀ 2m/2yd gold ribbon 6mm/¼in wide ❀ Craft knife
❀ 9 Carnations - instructions in flower section ❀ 13 Ivy leaves
❀ Last two items made into a spray, using green tape, with some ribbon loops.
❀ Piping bag of cream royal icing with No 1 tube ❀ No 2 piping tube.

IN ADVANCE
Using template, cut out the 2 sections of the card in pastillage and leave to dry flat. Once dry, secure together, using royal icing, over-pipe the join and along the edges of the card as completed picture shows.

TO DECORATE CAKE
1. Coat cake and secure to board.

2. Make a paper pattern for one side of the cake, fold and cut to give a scalloped shape. Using a ruler and pencil, mark off the top edge at 1cm/³⁄₈in intervals. Pin to cake.

3. Using a craft knife with the flat ribbon insertion blade, make a vertical cut at the 1cm/³⁄₈in marks.

4. Cut some ribbon into 1cm/³⁄₈in lengths and using the knife, push ribbon into one cut then push the other end into the next cut, continue all round cake as shown.

5. With royal icing and No1 tube pipe a shell border around the bottom edge of cake, then pipe a vertical shell shape between each shell as illustrated above.

6. Pipe three small dots at each point where ribbon goes 'into' the cake.

7. Using the quick flower paste rolled thinly, cut out the frill shape from the template at the back, then using the pointed end of a No 2 tube, cut three holes out of each scallop along the bottom of the frill.

8. Frill gently with a cocktail stick, and using water, stick into place around each corner under ribbon. Trim with gold bows as picture shows.

9. Secure card and flowers with royal icing. Note: If you do not feel confident enough to wire the spray together, place card on cake and fix, then add an extra lump of sugar paste between the card and paste and arrange the flowers, ribbons and leaves into this.

CELEBRATION CAKE

This cream and lavender cake is just perfect for the special person in your life.

YOU WILL NEED:
For a 30cm/12in trefoil cake on a 35cm/14in round cake board

❀ 1kg/2.2lb plus 125gm/4½oz ivory sugar paste (the same in marzipan for a fruit cake)
❀ 125gm/4½oz quick flower paste in lavender ❀ 125gm/4½oz quick flower paste in ivory
❀ 1m/1yd lavender ribbon 3mm/⅛in wide ❀ 1m/1yd cream ribbon 5cm/2in wide
❀ Piping bags of royal icing-one in lavender, one in ivory, each with a No 0 tube
❀ 7-9 orchids in lavender ❀ Frill cutter ❀ Crimper ❀ Silicone paper
❀ An assortment of small blossoms made from quick flower paste in various shades of
ivory, through to lavender.

IN ADVANCE
Coat cake board with ivory sugar paste and
trim with cream ribbon.

TO DECORATE CAKE
1. Coat cake with ivory sugar paste. Fix to
cake board with a little royal icing. Crimp
round bottom edge.

2. Using a pin or scriber and a ruler, go
around and mark cake 2cm/¾in and
3cm/1¼in from the bottom. (This is the
guide for the frills.)

3. Make a silicone paper template of one
section of the cake, the same size and height.
From the bottom edge, mark the position of
the frill, allow space for the lavender ribbon,
then trace above that line the pattern for the
embroidery (from back of book). Prick the
pattern through the paper as a guide for the
embroidery.

4. Using a garret frill cutter, cut out a
shape from thinly rolled quick flower
paste in lavender, remove the middle
piece. With a cocktail stick thin and frill
the outer edge.

5. Cut through and open into a
straight length.

6. Using water, fix into position
following the 2cm/¾in marks
on the cake.

7. Repeat in ivory, fixing the
frill on the higher 3cm/1¼in mark.

8. With a little royal icing fix ribbon in
position above the frill.

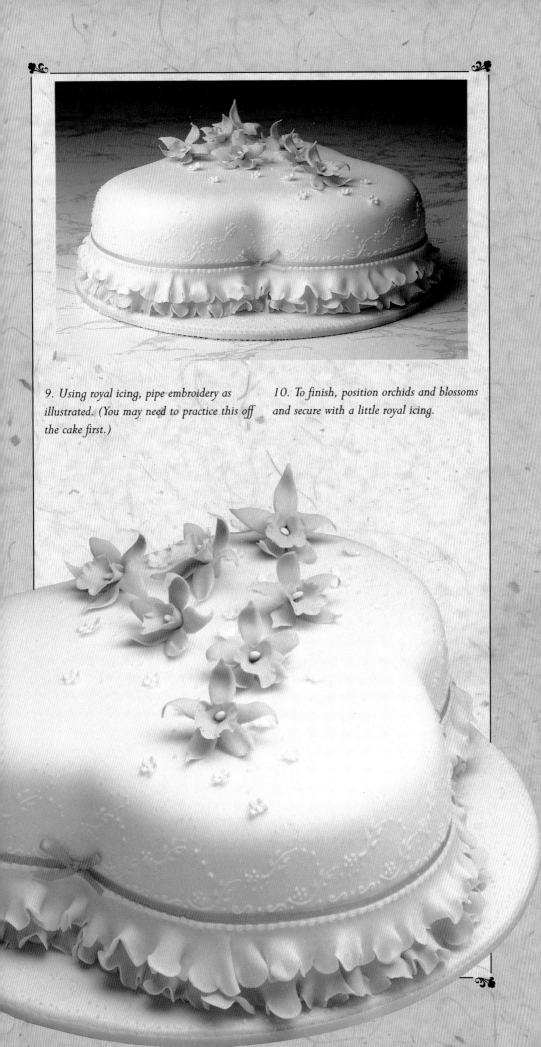

9. Using royal icing, pipe embroidery as illustrated. (You may need to practice this off the cake first.)

10. To finish, position orchids and blossoms and secure with a little royal icing.

SINGLE TIER WEDDING CAKE

This all white wedding cake is a classic, add colour and it would make an ideal Anniversary or Valentine's Day cake.

YOU WILL NEED:

✿ A 30cm/12in heart-shaped fruit cake coated in marzipan
and white royal icing on a 35cm/14in heart-shaped board
✿ 1m/1yd white ribbon 6mm/¼in wide.
✿ 1 mix of royal icing ✿ Piping bags ✿ Nos 1 and 6 piping tubes
✿ Patterns and templates from the back of the book
✿ Run-out film - or heavy cellophane paper

IN ADVANCE-On run-out film
1. Flood out the small hearts using the method described in the Teddy Bear's cake. You will need 4 large and 8 small ones.

2. To make the centre piece, first pipe the outside and dividing lines of the heart shape. Then fill in where indicated on template with cornelli type piping (See Step 4 opposite).

3. Flood in with soft icing where indicated on template. Leave to dry under a lamp. Leave for another two days before you move it, then peel it off the film.

4. Turn it over and flood in the back of the thick bands. Leave under lamp to dry. (You do not need to re-pipe the outer and dividing lines) This makes the top decoration double-sided.

5. Now run out a large heart-shaped plaque from the pattern and position the centrepiece on it. Take care to keep it propped up straight. Again, dry this initially under a lamp but leave for several days before you move it.

6. Flood the cake board with soft royal icing. Pipe rope edging in royal icing using No 6 tube and pipe fine line using No 1 tube.

TO DECORATE CAKE

1. Make a template pattern for the oval shapes on the cake and scribe pattern on.

2. With royal icing and No 1 tube, pipe a line for the oval shape, then pipe 2 more over the top to 'build up' the linework.

3. With No 6 tube, place 2 graduated ropes between each oval shape.

4. With No 1 tube, fill in the oval shapes with cornelli work (a series of Ws and Ms).

5. Pipe lines under the ropes and around them on the top of the cake.

6. Pipe a line down from between the ropes on the sides and fix a large heart into position-embellish with dots.

7. At the front and back, pipe two lines at an angle and fix a small heart on either side, again embellish with dots.

8. On the top, fix a heart between each of the graduated ropes.

9. Position the heart centrepiece and fix with royal icing.

AUTUMN CAKE

❀

A cake to warm the heart as winter approaches

YOU WILL NEED:

✿ 20cm/8in hexagonal cake-coated in dark cream, crimped around bottom edge
✿ 30cm/12in round cake board-also coated and edged with ribbon
✿ A piece of pastillage in brown, formed to resemble driftwood
✿ 5 blackberries at various stages of ripeness ✿ 4 blackberry flowers
✿ 15 bramble leaves in dark green using leaf cutter from pack ✿ 10-12 acorns
✿ Approximately 30 oak leaves made in various shades of brown
using template from back of book
✿ 125gm/4½oz quick flower paste in dark cream
✿ 3 pieces of dowel 3cm/1¼in diameter and 20cm/8in long
(plastic pillar centre rods are ideal)
✿ A little royal icing in a piping bag for fixing wood and leaves

TO DECORATE CAKE

1. With a piece of paper measure a strip the length of one side of the hexagon, roll out very thinly the paste for the drapes (1mm/¹⁄₃₂in thick) and cut a rectangle 10cm/4in deep and the length of the paper strip.

2. Take one piece of dowel and roll the top edge of the piece of cut paste under and around the dowel.

3. Repeat this with the bottom edge of the paste.

4. Take the third dowel and place under the paste between the other two, gently ease all three together, this will pleat the paste like fabric.

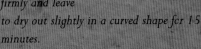

5. Remove the dowels, squeeze the ends of paste together firmly and leave to dry out slightly in a curved shape for 15 minutes.

6. To fix to cake, pick up drape and brush underside with water, position onto cake, hold in place for a minute to stick, repeat this for all sides.

7. To make the knot that covers the joins use a smaller piece of paste approximately 8cm/3¼in square, pleat with dowels as before, remove the dowels and turn both ends under, then moisten with water on the underside and place over joins immediately.

8. Arrange blackberries, flowers and bramble leaves into 2 small sprays.

9. Fix driftwood and sprays to the cake with royal icing.

10. Add acorns and oak leaves as picture shows, fixing them with royal icing.

TWO TIER WEDDING CAKE

This is a delightful design of roses and lace and a beautiful focal point for any wedding reception.

YOU WILL NEED:
✿ 30cm/12in fruit cake, petal shaped
✿ 15cm/6in fruit cake, petal shaped
Both coated with marzipan and ivory sugar paste,
placed on boards that are 5cm/2in larger and also
coated with ivory sugar paste, edged with ribbon.
✿ 3 Pillars ✿ 1 mix royal icing coloured ivory ✿ Piping bags and No 1 piping tubes
✿ Run-out film ✿ Sugar roses and blossoms - in the colour of your choice
✿ Ribbon to tone with flowers ✿ Green tape ✿ Cream wired Gypsophilia
✿ Lace patterns and template for the embroidery from back of book.

IN ADVANCE
To make sugar flowers-you will need:
✿ 6 Rose buds ✿ 7 Small roses
✿ 7 Large roses ✿50 Blossoms
✿ 21 Buds for blossoms ✿ Approximately
20 leaves ✿ Make ribbon loops-you will
need approximately 20 wired loops

Pipe lace by placing the pattern under the

*run-out film and with No 1 tube follow the
pattern and pipe the lines. Leave to dry.*

*To complete, let some royal icing down to a
flowing consistency as the run-outs on
Teddy Bear cake. Carefully flood in the
larger leaf patterned lace very thinly so that
the piped lines still show. Leave to dry.
Make plenty - you will need spares.*

TO DECORATE CAKE
*1. Immediately after coating and placing on
the boards, pipe a shell border using a No
1 tube.*

*2. Make a pattern for one section of each
cake and mark out positions for embroidery
and the line for lace all the way round. Prick
out design on cake with a pin.*

*3. With royal icing and No 1 tube, pipe the
embroidery. Pattern A above lace and pattern
B along the base.*

*4. Using a paint brush or very fine palette
knife, ease the lace off the film.*

*5. Place the dots of royal icing onto the cake
and stick the lace into position. You may find
it easier to place the top row first.*

*6. Now assemble the flower sprays. Using
florists' tape, start with a bud and gradually
work down the stem adding other blossoms,
ribbons, Gypsophilia, roses and leaves, to
make a thin line about 40cm/16in long.
Gently ease this into a circle and secure the
ends neatly.*

7. For the top tier you will need:
✿ 2 buds ✿ 3 small roses ✿ 3 large roses
✿ 6 small sprays of blossom made up of 2
buds and 3 flowers.

8. Starting in the centre, keeping the florists' tape in the same position under the central flowers, construct a round posy.

9. Position the pillars carefully on the bottom tier, inside the circle of flowers. You will need to use supports that go through the cake and up through the pillars to take the weight of the top tier.

YULE LOG

T was the night before Christmas and everyone was waiting for Santa ...

YOU WILL NEED:

❀ 500gm/1lb 2oz brown sugar paste ❀ 2 large Swiss roll cakes
❀ 30cm/12in square board coated with white sugar paste edged with red ribbon
❀ 10 holly leaves in green flower paste made using template at back of book
❀ 1 large holly leaf for sleeping mouse-flower paste
❀ A little marzipan for the heads of the mice in dark brown
plus a little light brown for sack ❀ A little red quick flower paste
❀ A little white quick flower paste ❀ A little pink and black quick flower paste
❀ A little white sugar paste ❀ Liquid food colour in brown, red and green
❀ Gum glue ❀ Half a mix of white royal icing

IN ADVANCE

1. Using templates cut out and vein 10 holly leaves and dry on crumpled kitchen paper to give natural shapes.

2. With red flower paste, make approximately 12 berries.

3. Cut out 1 large holly leaf and dry inside a round container (to hold sleeping mouse).

4. With red, make a small sausage for the body of Santa, cut a third of the way up to form legs.

5. Mould a pair of boots in black.

6. Make a hole in the bottom of each leg and stick the boot up into the hole using gum glue.

7. Make a thin strip of white and stick all the way round above the legs to represent the bottom of the tunic, then take this up the centre.

8. Add a thin strip of black for the belt. Make the buckle from a square of white paste.

9. In marzipan, mould the head. Take a large ball and roll into a cone. Make two indentations for eyes. Take two small balls of brown and two small balls of pink. Place the pink on top of the brown. With a bone tool, press the two together then fix into place for the ears. Pipe white royal icing into the eye sockets. Stick a tiny ball of pink onto the end of the cone to form a nose. When eyes are dry, paint the irises.

10. To fix the head into position, insert a piece of dry spaghetti into the body leaving enough to go into the head.

11. Make two small red sausages for the arms, form two 'hands' in white and fix into the arms as with the boots.

12. With glue, stick arms into position, add a cuff of white fur to each arm and a collar of white fur. Leave Santa to dry completely. You may need to prop the arms. Add a tail.

13. Mould a sack shape in pale brown marzipan. Add a dark brown tie and fill with little moulded parcels.

14. For the sleeping mouse, place a mound of sugar paste into the large leaf and add a small pillow above it. Roll out a thin blanket of white sugar paste and paint with food

colours. Cover mound, and fold back.

15. Mould a small mouse head as before and stick into position, but for the eyes, make two small balls of brown marzipan, cut off bottom section and glue into sockets. This gives the impression of closed eyes.

16. Mould 2 small marzipan paws and fix, then add a tail to come from under the blanket.

TO DECORATE CAKE

1. Cut Swiss rolls to form a log shape and coat with brown sugar paste. Paint on dark brown log markings. Place on prepared board.

2. Spread thin royal icing over to represent snow as shown in the picture.

3. Position holly leaves and berries and fix with royal icing.

4. Fix models as picture shows.

CONCLUSION

We do sincerely hope you enjoy using this book. Combine ideas from different projects and the cakes you can produce will be many and varied. You can change colours or adapt the modelled flowers into an almost infinite variety of decoration. The stamens supplied with the pack enable even more flowers to be created, use them with the primrose flower instructions to make blossoms of different colours.

Good luck and happy cake decorating.

TEDDY BEAR CAKE

BUTTERFLY

CRIMPER PATTERN

CHRISTENING CAKE

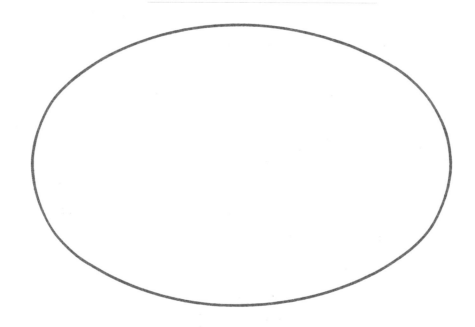

CORNER PATTERN FOR DRAPE

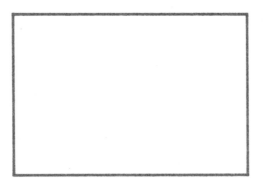

CRIB BASE, DRY OVER CURVE

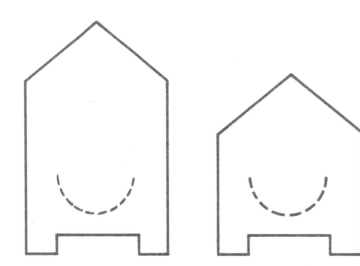

CRIB ENDS

PRIMROSE CAKE

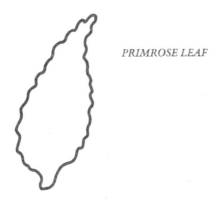

PRIMROSE LEAF

LACE PATTERN

GEOMETRIC CAKE

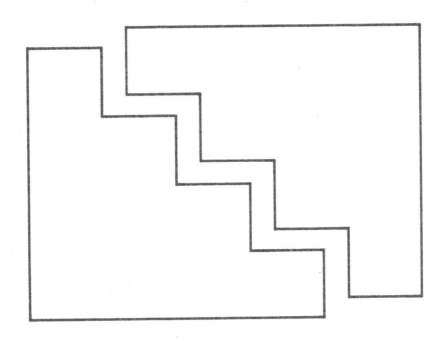

SIDE PANELS FOR GEOMETRIC CAKE-CUT 4 OF EACH IN PASTILLAGE

(NOTE) Scale up to size if larger cake used.

CLOWN CAKE

YULE LOG   GOLDEN WEDDING CAKE

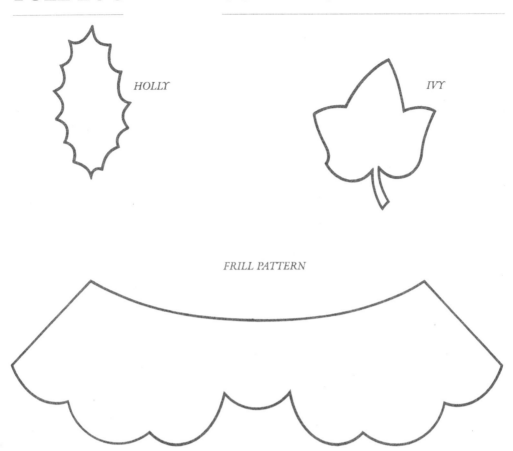

HOLLY

IVY

FRILL PATTERN

CARD PATTERN, CUT ONE COMPLETE, CUT ONE WITH HOLE

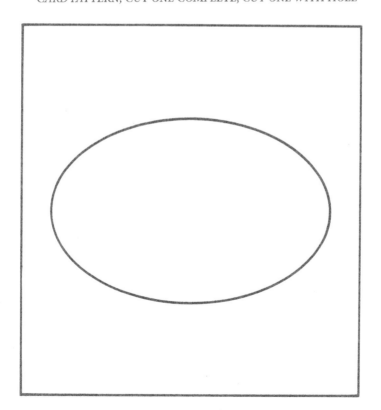

CELEBRATION CAKE

EMBROIDERY PATTERN

QUICK ORCHID

BACK

CENTRE PETAL ORCHID

CENTRE PETAL CATTLEYA ORCHID

CATTLEYA ORCHID

TOP

SINGLE TIER WEDDING CAKE

PATTERN FOR RUN-OUT
PLAQUE ON TOP OF CAKE

- - - - - - - - - - - - - - - -

position of upright heart

HEARTS FOR SIDE AND TOP
DECORATION

TWO TIER WEDDING CAKE

LACE-top row

LACE-bottom leaf-patterned row

Embroidery pattern A

Embroidery pattern B

ASSORTED TEMPLATES

LARGE BLOSSOM

CALYX

OAK LEAVES